Bachelard Interpreted 3

Real Weight

Frank Prem

Wild Arancini Press
2025

Publication Details

Title: Real Weight: Bachelard Interpreted Book 3
ISBN: 978-1-923166-25-7 (p-bk)
ISBN: 978-1-923166-22-6 (e-bk)

Published by Wild Arancini Press
Copyright © 2025 Frank Prem
All rights reserved.

No part of this publication may be reproduced, stored in a retrieval system, or transmitted in any form or by any means, electronic, mechanical, photo-copying, recording or otherwise, without prior written permission from the publisher and author.
A catalogue record for this book is available from the National Library of Australia.

Cover Concept: Wild Arancini Press
Cover Image AI assistant: Adobe Firefly

The earth provides.

CONTENTS

Real Weight

Introduction 1

Earth and Reveries of Repose

to find repose 5
curiosity 8
all is 10
the element of doubt 11
almost 13
indigo (a dyer's hands) 16
ink (for fire) 18
closer 20
purity (inner) 21
the labyrinth 23
crossroads 24
into the eye (of the serpent) 27
out of place (in the jungle dream) 29
an object worthy 31
danger: writing 32
an observation (at the last) 34
scaling 35
her potential 37
the cup to quench (by subtle water) 39

Earth and Reveries of Will

real weight 43
a literary image 45
between two words (1) 47
the line of thirteen 48

between two words (2)	50
inside the poem	51
trans	52
cubed	54
the yes: the no	55
loam poem	56
sword	58
re-genesis	60
the life in it	62
in the workshop	65
practical violence	67
adjustment of the heart of the earth	68
the professor, on an ambiguity	70
perceiving the image is just a chance	72
should I need a light	74
the air-craft of kitchen utensils	76
two bowls	78
fare	81
the accident of the kitchen sponge	83
hunger	86
he himself	88
hands of me	91
a frenchman abroad (the appreciation)	93
five elements of a loaf of bread	96
fermenting the plate	97
strength of porcelain	99
factory work	101
stoking	104
shaping class (no preconceptions)	106
to paint (like a master)	108
the fore-running dream (how to live an orderly day)	111

different storm	114
reverie of the woodman	115
by braille	117
the hand	120
resistance	121
a little skunk	122
the beach	124
a viscous dough	126
within the dough	128
grounding of a poet by friend	129
light (too heavy)	132
a voice of dust	134
closed: barefoot	136
hammer/smith	138
swirl dance	139
halving the stone with love	140
tuning	141
rules in the hands of the god (of war)	143
filled with	146
three hammers	148
nerves of steel	151
reverie on a state (of being nothing)	153
new tongs for the maker	155
tempering	157
to appease	158
the temper of steel	160
the cauteriser	161
make you (like iron)	163
paint your name	164
I breathe a dancer	165
the night forge	166

necessary sacrifice	167
a vengeance	168
rock-lan roll	171
chasm	172
the long dream	174
the wind (on Easter Island)	176
hard rock	178
sisyphus speaks	179
old (lithic) hurts	181
fred's backdrop	182
joyous	185
oneiric research (preparing to dream)	187
murmur	188
the miner reflects on his mountain deep	189
colours of the great work	193
introvert medicine	194
bridging mine	195
the incomplete findings of the dream reviewer	196
diamond and star	198
the contemplation	200
the suddenness of a change (of voices)	202
where *I* may be	203
Bachelard Source Materials	207
Author Information	209
Other Published Works	211
What Readers Say	213

Real Weight

Introduction

French scientist and philosopher Gaston Bachelard (1884 - 1962) explored and examined poetics and poetry in great depth over the course of his lifetime, particularly examining the poetics of natural elements, of which he identified the four that are traditionally considered:

Fire
Water
Air
Earth

In addition, however, he (effectively) identified two further elements, or dimensions, for his examination:

Time
Space

The *Bachelard Interpreted* poetry series responds to each of these elements and dimensions, as well as encompassing some of Bachelard's further scientific and literary interests.

Real Weight considers the poetic aspects of earth. Its malleability and resistance. The capacity to endure all that comes through millennia on millennia.

The collection engages with the making of things from the earth - food, art, livelihood. It acknowledges the necessity to find and to know the good earth.

Note: *Real Weight* is one of a series of poetry collections inspired by the work of Gaston Bachelard. References to the Bachelard translations that have been relied on as source materials for this project are listed at the end of this book.

Earth and Reveries of Repose

to find repose

the earth spoke

> *come*
>
> *come*
> *and rest with me*
>
> *deep in your heart*
> *you know*
>
> *I*
> *await you*

but
he looked down
into
the darkened depths

said

> *no no*
> *no*
>
> *that is*
> *much too deep*
>
> *for me*

the blaze of the fire
called out

> *come to me*
>
> *I*
> *will dance for you*
>
> *for you*

> we
> will dance

but he knew
he could
never stand that heat

did not wish
to burn

and when the wind
said

> I
> will sing you
> a song
>
> a lullaby
> that knows
> your name

he replied
courteously

> no
> no I cannot hear that
>
> your breeze is chill
> your breath
> is filled
> with shivers
>
> no no

at the water's edge
the laughter rang

he knew
he would find no peace

Real Weight

no calm
in
running rills

    no

instead
he turned
into himself

into
his mind

finally

finally
repose

curiosity

to see
beyond the skin
he sliced
the flesh
with his sharpened
knife

    the welling
    red –
    that slowly turned
    to brown –
    he washed
    aside

    noting
    the dispersal
    through the water

to see
beyond the meat
he cut

exposing
a tendon
to the air

    the string
    that could move
    a finger
    on his hand

    noting
    the clear
    come hither

Real Weight

to see
beyond the gristle
lying there
he cut down
to reach the bone

> *tapped*
> *the blade*
>
> *tok*
>
> *tok*
>
> *saw the red*
> *on white*
>
> *nicked it with*
> *the blade point*
>
> *thought*
>
> *this needs . . .*
>
> *. . . what this really needs*
> *is a saw*

he wrapped his arm

wandered out
into the shed

searching
again

all is . . .

I dive
into the centre

I feel no ending
there

all
is plunge

all
is fall

all is
deeper . . .

and
deeper yet

in the heart
there is *still*
the heart
waiting
to be found

the element of doubt

the paper was white

she could see
that

white
is white

> *but why . . .*

she wondered

> *. . . why?*

is it as simple
as

> *because!*

or
is white
a relative thing

white
because it contains
black

a contrast
seen
in the absence
of its opposite

> *how . . .*

she asked herself

*. . . how
do I know
this
to be white?*

*this
as it is?*

I *believe*
it has depth

I believe
it is *black*
just
under

beneath

its skin

almost

brothers

they were
almost
twins

nature . . .

> given time
>
> given the working
> of her ways

. . . nature
can accomplish
anything

~

> he was moulded
> from clay
> to
> flesh
>
> breathed
> to life
>
> to move his limbs
>
> into his mouth
> so
> he could speak
>
> he was moulded

~

he was shaped

out of
silica

from
the quartz

blown
to man-like
by the eroding
wind

sculpted
to perfection

his mouth
his lips
his nose and eyes

arms and legs
and
his torso

silent

immobile

perfection

he
was shaped

~

sometimes
in the afternoon
as the sun
subsided

he grew
lonely

Real Weight

sat on the plinth

rested

against his brother
for comfort

a small comfort

~

they
were twins

almost
twins

indigo (a dyer's hands)

my hand is
blue

my hand
is green

my nails
shellac-harden
my skin . . .

leather

I am so much
leather

all my creases
marked
in red

every pore
the rainbow
every pore
its own

like the hand
of the philosopher
and his multi-coloured
fragment
my hands
hold the power
of every hue
they make

ha
look *there*

I have smeared
the darkness
upon my chest

Real Weight

small matter

no matter

it is always
my hands
that squeeze

today

you may call me
indigo

ink (for fire)

she leaned across
the hearth

almost
near enough
to the small flame —
and the red
and black
coals —
to burn herself

beaker
in one hand

stopper
in the other

she
engaged
in the delicate art
of smoke

of trapping the smoke
within
her bottle

art
it was

art it is

for having trapped
the wavering substance
in sufficient quantity

and reeking now
from the fumes
and from
the fire

Real Weight

her task
is to undertake
distillation
of the dye . . .

out of the smoke . . .

into ink

it is her intention
this day
to write —
in ash and ichor —
all
the characters
of fire

closer

it was the cave
with the glow worms
that drew her

into the watching —
deep
almost solid —
darkness

starred
by the pointillist

fluorescence
of a thousand
heedless
specks of light

that illuminated
nothing

here
she could gaze
on the vast universe

brought close

purity (inner)

in the same way
that he sought
the true sulphur
that lit
the true fire

he searched
for purity

outside?

the surface?

> *yes yes*
>
> *soap*
>
> *water*
>
> *clean*

but
what of the inside

how might it be possible
to purify
within

> *a true*
> *soap?*
>
> *a true*
> *water?*

he did not
know

but like the smell
of essential brimstone

the idea
hung
at the edges of his mind

the solution
at the very boundary
of his sight

like the dream
of gold
from lead

he aspired to purity
located
inner

the labyrinth

go left
at the first
three turns

turn right

turn now

go left
at the next three turns

turn
right
now

and turn
turn again

turn
into the heart

go left
at the first three turns
then
go back
to the
beginning

crossroads

(1)

a crossing
of roads

I wonder
where I'm going

no believer
in the map
nor
the plan
am I

a stumble
or
a firm step . . .

each
may lead falsely

I mark them
as places

my places
en route

dust and stone
and wheel ruts
run
ninety degrees
to left and to right

mud-brown and sludge
and deeper wheel ruts
on the straight
lead
to a horizon

Real Weight

where have I been . . .

. . . am I going

*will I
even be
alive*

*at the crossing
of my life*

*I wonder
where
am I headed*

so
I close my eyes
turn myself around
in a circle

one way . . .

any
way

is the way
for me to go

I follow
in the wheel ruts

the deep and dusty
wheel ruts
of another pilgrim
already
passed by

~

(2)

I ask myself

>   *where*
>   *does this road*
>   *go*
>
>   *or*
>   *this road*
>
>   *or*
>   the other

only the wind
whispers
an answer

only the wind

it is gone
and I
did not hear it
leave
me
behind

into the eye (of the serpent)

the serpent
lifts its head

I draw back
against my will

I don't want
that tongue
to taste me

the air
is a treachery
that carries me
on the breeze

and soon . . .

soon . . .

I am swaying

bending

soon . . .

soon . . .

I am deep
in serpent eyes

it has found me

> *I have no wings*
> *to fly*
>
> *I have no legs*
> *to run*
>
> *I am the ripple*
> *etched*
> *across the sands*

and soon . . .

soon . . .

I am swaying

into a stony eye

a stony serpent eye

>   *I need no wings*
>   *to fly*
>
>   *I need no legs*
>   *to run*

the tongue
flickers

out of place (in the jungle dream)

each vine
becomes
its own snake

it writhes
before the wind
can blow

I hear the cold breath
hissing

this thicket
is up
as high as
the sky

dark sun
no stars at night
every footfall shrills

hello

in a high-pitched voice
and tremor

go on . . .

I will go on
in a tentative braille

feeling
with my feet
for the prospect
of a fall

arms out wide . . .

out wide and blind
touch twitching

day is night
is day
is
all the same
to me

here I am
where the pythons
sing their songs

I hear nothing

I see nothing

I
am nothing

Real Weight

an object worthy

a thing
becomes an object
worthy
of my meditation
when I
choose it

to meditate
upon

danger: writing

as she wrote
it came to life

she started the thought
of a body

coiled

one coil
upon another one

her idea
was adorned
in coloured scales
that glimmered —
glinted —
in the light

ruby red
and diamond clear

emerald

as she wrote the sun
to warm
a ripple
spread

    around
    and around

she wrote it strong

    and around

enough to tell
in just a glance

    and around

Real Weight

the danger there

the head —
of *course* —
a triangular

ever present

>*the testing*

>*the tasting*

>*the tongue*

lastly
the eyes

and
as she wrote them
they fixed on her

began
to sway

an observation (at the last)

she had time
to notice
as the serpent
continued
in a
serial
circumnavigation
of her
that it seemed
to wish
to
need
to touch her
with
every
part
of its body
and it was
only
when the last
the least
tip
of its tail
embraced her
that it
began
slowly
to squeeze

scaling

a thin man

lean
like someone
who only eats
a little
once in a while

patient
and nonchalant
he picks up —
both gentle and firm —
each snake

each asp

each serpent
as it twines

    too close

    too tight

    too much

moves it
to one side

he squats
beside the basket
unblinking

when he moves
it is a graceful
movement

languorous
as a sway

fast
as a whiplash

in certain light . . .

and
under certain
sun

it is possible to see
the abrasive
roughness
of his condition

for he is naked —
near naked —
where he squats

each day
scaling
a little more

her potential

when she stood still
just
for a moment

movement
could be seen

a stirring
in the earth
beneath . . .
. . . around
her feet

then
she would wriggle
her toes
a little

reposition her feet
in a sort of
shuffle

before stepping away

always
a little further away
from a minor disturbance
of the earth
in the vicinity

one day
she did not move

>   *would not move*
>   *could not move*

I don't know

her feet —
maybe —
took a liking
to the loam

ecstasy

in a rapture
she closed her eyes
the better
to feel

as roots
went down

entering the earth

of course
it's obvious now

she was not a woman
at all

always
she was
the *potential*
to be a tree

the cup to quench (by subtle water)

I make this wine
with subtle water

pick —
one by one —
the stars
to tread

steeped
with the breath
of a comet passing

let this cup

my demons
quench

Earth and Reveries of Will

real weight

is it real
when you *see* it

because you see it

is it real
if you
are not *there*

and
is it real
when you *dream* it

if you *imagine*

is it only real
then
while you stay sleeping

do you have to stroke it
with your fingers

can you explore it
inside your mind

when you dream it
is it just a memory

or can you
conjure
a thing that
no-one has seen before

is there a scale . . .

a way to weigh
the real thing

let's measure up
each point of view

does the *real*
that you can see
and hold
outweigh the lightness
of a caress
within a dream

a literary image

here

look

I'm going to draw this . . .

something
you've never seen
before

I'll give it
a round face . . .

eyes and ears

a bendy nose
like yours

it looks a little —
I think —
like you
but . . .

what about
a shaggy mane

a long loop
of tail

how many limbs

yes
four

or five

and
I think I'll draw it
in a pond

with a water lily —
dripping —
on its head

hmmm
I still think
there's a resemblance
to you

ah
never mind
I was only joking

really

I was just trying to make a picture
out of words

between two words (1)

between two words
that rhyme
lies the metaphor

> *like the magpie*
> *and its song*
>
> *like*
> *a round of firewood*
> *and the blade*
> *of my axe*

there
the image
unfolds
in its personal melody

> *the ballad moves me*
> *to the high country*
> *when I close*
> *my eyes*
>
> *I sing the mountains*
>
> *blue*
> *the valleys*
>
> *my story*

so tell it
like a tale in a song
revealed
by the in-between place
and time
of two words
that rhyme

the line of thirteen

today she read
a line

in the book
on the page

somewhere
close to the centre

an average line
of thirteen words
or fourteen

ebb and flow
from the start
. . .
to the end
. . .

she pondered
the beauty of words
arranged by typeset

in a straight line
pressed across the page

she thought it
good

it left her
warm

after a contemplation
she could almost
countenance
reading another

a serious temptation
but . . .

Real Weight

no
thirteen words
laid out as a thing
of beauty
is enough

best to put aside
the page
the book
and to ponder again
what she has read

anticipate
the words to come
tomorrow

it is *so*
exciting

between two words (2)

the first word sang
like a bell —
struck clean —
in the morning

and the sound
ran through
the clusters
and the cloisters
and the phrases
all along the line
until
the last word
sang

the memory of images
shaped by the sound
of a bell-
struck clean —
by the first word
of morning

inside the poem

what is the inside
of a poem

are you there
if you live it

do you have to know
or *is* it
anyway

~

what is the inside
of your life

do you reside
in stanzas

must you recite yourself
or are you
because you

~

your image has
a lyric flow

your life is rhythm
rhyme

your world
the driven cadence

how is it
living
on the inner side

come read to me

your life
aloud

trans

he turned his eyes away
then
let them return

he could see no difference
no change

from image in his mind
to writing on the page
he had lost
the sense of it

groups of lines
side-by-side
one
on top of the other
without meaning

perhaps

he wondered

perhaps
he might move them
around
treat them
like a puzzle

this block
over to there

that block above

below

move them around
move them around
desperately
move them

Real Weight

until he could read
the tale

until it made sense

until it was the image
that he saw
inside his mind
before he took up
his pen
to write

cubed

he placed a cube
of sugar
in a glass of water
watched it slowly
melt away

he placed a cube of sugar
in a glass of water
watched it slide around
on a surface
of ice
he twirled the glass
to a clinking sound

he placed
a cube of sugar
where water
had bubbled in a glass
watched it disappear
as though
it had never been there
at all

nothing stays the same
not even the time
it takes

the yes: the no

harden my heart
say

    no

soften my stance
say

    yes

change my mind
like water from the block

harden
soft
in the centre

resistance
is rejection

acceptance
is to yield

I am stamping
in firm steps
I am
on the tips of toes

who can decipher
between the hard
and the soft

who knows
the way to go

loam poem

she walked
with a shovel
to the garden

identified
the waiting bed

leaned towards her task
and dug
began an opening stanza

overturned
the sod and soil
arranged into lines
that she could speak
from left to right
across the bed

her page

and the poem she dug
read straight
and neat

its subject was springtime
and growing

to every phrase
that her spade turned in
she added viable contemplations
of seed

> *her beans to be*
>
> *the peas she thought*
>
> *carrots and brown onion*

Real Weight

ode

to garden

song of the table

as she finished her composition
and the garden square
her mind turned
towards the sequel

another bed
of lines to score

this time
by a metal rake
dragged through dirt
and loam
into another representation
of her heart

another poem

sword

it was never his intention
to resist
but . . .

sometimes . . .

a blow
will only achieve
indentation

sometimes . . .

desire alone
will not
yield itself
into a predetermined
shape

the hammer
is merely
a blunt-form instrument

a rod of metal
is merely an aspect
of potential

the artisan
is an artist
now
of positivity and force
in equal measure

the arm . . .

the descending strike
of *one-on-one* . . .

is a rhythm
of hard love
for this creation

Real Weight

fire in the forge
a passion

the plunge
into cold water

again . . .

boiled to steam

his
is the temper
of the steel

he
is the sword

re-genesis

do not fear
I will not
destroy you

the words
of reassurance
spoken aloud
crackled from the coals

my aim is only to transform
I seek to change you
from what is now
to what
might yet be

have faith in me
I am your friend

seek reverie
and rest
within the crucible
while I do what I must do

and change . . .

change you will

hot
soft
aglow
running red

the heart of what you are

when you are
flow
you will
again

Real Weight

*you will
anew
poured
into a shape
you must snug close
to the moulding walls*

*you will cool
I shall depart*

*in your new
you will be*

the words
crackled aloud
by coals

the life in it

in truth
she had allowed herself
a small indulgence

a little mindless
contemplation
while she worked
the knife

the narrow chisel

it always came on her
that way

as though the job
did not require
her active thought
merely
her presence
somewhere behind the clever-work
of her hands

the root
had been formed
into a gnarl
shaped
into a character
that she could discern . . .

could elaborate

a shapely knob
she could position
at the end of a stick

a lady's walking stick

her work today
was delicate

cleaning with the knife

Real Weight

scraping

shaping with fine touches
of the chisel

but at no point
imposing herself . . .

her will
on the form
that she sought
to release

the character
was already present

in place

only requiring her
subtle
exposure

and so
there was no room
for her thinking self
to become involved
when hands —
with their sensitive fingers
upon the wood
and knowing grip
on the tools —
could work so much better
without her

in her contemplation
she daydreamed
of walks overland

climbing gentle slopes
ambling along
to the cheerful sounds
of a small watercourse

herself
and the dog

and today's stick

she wouldn't ever do it
of course
it was just a daydream
and the stick
would be sold

but she felt . . .

believed really

that her dreaming —
while her hands were busy
and the shape emerged
beneath them —

put *life*

heart

and *purpose*

into the work
that she did

in the workshop

he was a man
who dreamed
within the tooled space
of his workshop

there
among the chisels and mallets

handsaws and planes

the sandpaper
and dust

he would find himself
in reverie

his hand —

a hairy-backed
thing of strength —
had only to run
idly
along the length
of a piece
of aged blackwood
or salvaged walnut

ash
or fiddle-backed redgum

and he would begin
to dream
the ways to shape it

the things he might craft
while minimising
any waste
of precious material

so hard to come by
now

his dreams were rich
filled with the deep wood colours
and the smells
of stain
and of polish

at home
his personal cabinetry
was thin stuff
chipboard and veneer

laminate plastic
on top of artificial wood

his bed
was mattress
on base

plastic wheels

no wood

at night
when sleep came
he would dream restlessly
in a toss and turn
of near agitation

becoming more tired
as the night progressed

relief would come
with the light of morning
and the prospect
of another day
of wood
and dreams
in the workshop

practical violence

he is not
a violent man
but . . .

with the bastard rasp
in his hand
there is a violence
within him

he leans
into the task
with everything that he has

and with each
shrill
stroke
he gouges
a curled shaving

a splintered
shining
fragment

and with each hungry drive
the rasp
is biting

and the victim
pared —
just a little —
back

but
he is not a violent man
and the viciousness
of his strikes
are all in the cause
of a practical
beauty

adjustment of the heart of the earth

      ziff   *ziff*   *ziff*   *ziff*

it is rhythmic
an almost squeal
pitched in high register

      ziff   *ziff*   *ziff*   *ziff*

the sound of metal
removing metal

      ziff   *ziff*

a pause
beneath the artificial brightness
cast by a naked fluoro lamp
as the exposed glare —
shining proud —
of *copper*
brass
steel

is removed from the jaws
of the metalwork vice
for examination
by hand and eye

tested for size
and fit
and sharpness of edges
before

      ziff   *ziff*   *ziff*   *ziff*

Real Weight

the process of adjustment
goes on

     ziff   *ziff*   *ziff*   *ziff*

grinding down
to the heart
of the metal

to the heart
of the earth

the professor, on an ambiguity

>well

he said

with the air
of an authority
on the subject at hand

>*what you are looking at*
>*is a twisted*
>*ambiguity*

>*yes*

>*yes*

>*that —*
>*I believe —*
>*is what it is*

>*you see*
>*this is a knotty problem*
>*which is*
>*plainly*
>*contorted*
>*and hardened*
>*to the point of being*
>*unresolvable*

>*knotty*
>*oh yes*

>*the knot itself*
>*however*
>*is —*
>*I must agree —*
>*it is hard*
>*but*
>*with a . . .*

Real Weight

[SNIP]

*. . . of my shears
not only is the knot
not –
so to speak
(ho ho) –
but
it becomes two
from one*

ambiguous indeed

he placed the two segments
on the table

studied them
for a moment
then
looked around the room

blinking

perceiving the image is just a chance

I chanced upon
an image
that I perceived
was something buried
deep inside me

like
the seed
of a thing

so I burrowed down
within myself
to knock and tap
and rattle

to search
from underneath
my miner's cap
for a way
to see inside . . .

some sort of door

it rattled
and it shook
and split itself
wide open

then sent a shoot
up
like a plant
kept in darkness
questing suddenly
for sun

up and up
and up we went
until light of day
kissed the bud tip

Real Weight

until the sun
coaxed it
to open
so I could gaze
on what I'd found

I chanced
upon an image

I perceived
that it was mine

I burrowed
deep inside myself
searching

I awakened there
something sleeping

the magic
of a chance
of an image
inside me
right now

should I need a light

the sun does not shine
inside a dream

the light there
comes from
an inner glow

it comes from
a *presumption*
of vision

of sight

how about that?

I see a dream
I am
in
the dream

I can see *that*
but
the sun
does not shine

its rays
are too hard

its rays
are too fierce

they would burn
the imagery

they would spear through
the dream
into my wakefulness

.
.
.

Real Weight

I
keep a torch
at my bedside

I keep it filled
with soft light
in case . . .

just
in case
there is a time

a night

in case there is
a dream
filled entirely
with my darkness

no inner glow

no sun

I keep a torch
beside my bed
for when I
am sleeping

just in case
I dream

the air-craft of kitchen utensils

father to son

a whistled gifting
of skills

all down the line

here

> *a set of knives*
> *sharpened on the wind*
>
> *singing*
> *knife songs*
> *to the clouds*
>
> *seeking the right pitch*
> *to slice*
> *right through the breeze*

there

> *four flat plates*
> *transparent clear*
>
> *packed dense*
> *to contain a meal*
> *of substance*
>
> *perhaps a steak*
>
> *a roast potato*
>
> *floating*
> *as though nothing*
> *tethers them underneath*

Real Weight

unravelled
with a blow
of warm air
from your mouth
no need to wash them
no earthly need
to store

just let them go

just let them blow

into the element
from which they came

let them blow

father
to son

a gifting of skills

useful utensils
whistled
from the air

two bowls

a bowl of dirt

> *a bowl of water*

from a cup
on her working table
she poured
a little water

> *he tipped*
> *a small quantity*
> *of garden soil*

that gave
a little splash

> *that dispersed*
> *as though it was cloud*

then drowned

taken into the tilth
of the soil

> *leaving behind*
> *a shading*
> *of darkness*

she poured more
until the dirt
became
like treacle

> *he tipped more*
> *the water*
> *embodied*

Real Weight

oozing through fingers
like warmed plasticine

> *running through his fingers*
> *like a slipping*
> *of pliant clay*

she poured more
until it was
a wash of slurry

> *he tipped more*
> *until*
> *there was no water*

a sienna shine
in the light
and sliding

> *just a damp mound*
> *of dirt*
> *and an empty cup*

she poured more

> *he tipped more*

dirty water

> *dirt*
> *only dirt*
>
> *no sign of water*

slipping through her fingers
falling
to an elongated splash
of droplets

squeezed through his fingers
it barely held form

falling into itself
again

serene
espresso brown

a rattle of dirt
reaching dirt

settled
into a water bowl

fare

what baker
had such hands

what baker
worked
such a flour

what baker
so absorbed
by her working

what baker
could knead any
more

what dough
ever rose
so high

what dough
loved the dough-maker more

what dough
would never
stop growing

what dough
what yeast
and
what more

what oven
could burnish a glaze
so golden

and what oven
ever held
such a heart

oh what oven
cooked buns
just as a sideline

what oven
could crust
thick enough
to contain

what bread is this
to serve at a table

what bread is this
to break into small

and what bread can this be
to inhale
so much butter
still warm from the oven
a soft kiss
in its touch

what fare
what fare is this

oh
what fare

the accident of the kitchen sponge

he held in his hand
a sponge

a very good sponge
shaped square
and coloured
yellow

kept on a shelf
beneath the sink
in the kitchen

he applied
an edge —
only an edge —
to an overflow

an accidental
spillage
of coffee
heedlessly sloshed
from his cup
onto the table

he was careless

the sponge
did its work . . .

a magic
of absorption

from the table
into the edge
that was the sponge

by accident —
so it seemed —
he moved the sponge
a small distance

centred it
over the spill

where it worked
more
sponge magic

an absorption

a drip —
at the end of a tap
in the laundry —
disappeared

the glass
that held jonquils —
so yellow
so bright —
suddenly dry

a pool of water
outside —
left behind
by the rain —
was smaller

was *gone*

the tremulous note
in the call of frogs
down at the creek
seemed
more strident

a cloud
that drifted the sky
as billowed cumulus
thinned
into cirrus transparency . . .

into blue

Real Weight

and the sponge —
seeming unable
to quite hold
the last liquid drops
of the spillage
of coffee —

grew larger

and
larger

hunger

the stranger was lost
anyone could see
that

everyone could see that

it was
almost amusing
to watch him lurch
and stumble

approaching people
one after another to ask

>   *where am I?*

>   *what is happening
>   to me?*

while being touched —
ritually —
by each new person
in turn

>   *ohhh*

said one

>   *mmm*

another

at each contact
a little more
unsteady

a little more lost

a lot more bewildered

Real Weight

ritual touching
by each new person
in turn

who then stood
a little straighter

smiled
a little easier

laughed
the sweet laughter
of release

all of them
somehow a little
fuller
after the contact

the stranger . . .

less

more lost

when he had given
all he had

when he was
totally
demented

he collapsed
breathing as though
in a fever

knowing nothing

knowing only
that he did not want
to be touched
anymore

he himself

he searched
among the textbooks
of his father's library
but found nothing

he looked at his face
reflected by his mother's mirror . . .

just a face
that's all

he cut himself
with a pointed blade

the sharp bite
drew blood

he watched it
haste onto his skin
then fall —
as water will fall —
then congeal

he studied —
for a while —
the animals

dogs and frogs
the chicken

the cat
as it purred beneath
his stroking fingers

and still
all he knew
was the *absence*
of any answers

Real Weight

he knew
that he didn't know
that
s all

in the garden . . .

mixing soils
digging holes
and planting seed

worthy
so worthy

all these other things
but
what about *him*
what about *himself*
how could he be sure
he was even
right there

know
the things
that would prove it

that he was *real*

it was enough
to make him mad
angry

insane

and all he knew
when he calmed himself
was that he had
to keep searching

that
the need to find
himself
might be the proof
the *only* proof

maybe alone
was all that there is
to being
uniquely
he

hands of me

my hand is
me

look at my palm
open
to the lines
of a lifetime

my hand is me

creases run
up the flesh
of my fingers

hatch marks and softness

deep lines
that are
what I have been

my hand is me

smooth skin
stretched
over my knuckles

a shape
that is hard
as a bone

only scars
and creases
alongside the place
where a finger curls
into one edge
of a fist

my hand is me

when I open my hand —
palm down —

stiffened fingers

tendons
veins
and pucker lines

who else
but me?

and
my hands

a frenchman abroad (the appreciation)

he said

> *it is perhaps*
>
> > *une coutume française*
>
> *a french thing —*
> *a conceit*
> *you know —*
> *to appreciate*
> *the golden crust so*
>
> *bread . . .*
>
> *the leavened loaf*
> *long sticks*
> *and buns still warm*
> *from the intensity*
> *of the oven*
>
> *a frenchman*
> *maybe*
> *appreciates these images*
> *the most*
>
> *and the smell*
> *the sense of it*
> *for him*
> *may be triggered*
> *by a picture*
>
> *the smell*
> *in its turn*
> *marks an image*
> *in the mind*
>
> *it is a*
> *foolish thing*
> *perhaps*

he said

> *but*
> *I*
> *am far from home*
> *living among*
> *(forgive me*
> *mon cher)*
>
> *living among*
> *the barbarians*

with an embarrassed

> *tchaa!*

he pulled open a drawer
at the front
of the dresser . . .

a folio
of photographs

a *baguette*
entire

a broken
pain
au levain

steam rising from
the *bâtard*
of an unknown
boulangerie
back home

a *boule*
on a cutting board

beignets
the bowl filled
to overflowing

Real Weight

    it is a
    french thing

he said

    a conceit

    no . . .

    an appreciation!

five elements of a loaf of bread

from the earth —
wheat grown —
the flour

add water

knead and pound
quarter turn
to knead and pound

let the air penetrate

a sexual thing

penetrate and rise
to fill the dough
and rise to —
almost —
overflow the bowl
where it is supposed
to be resting

a quarter turn
pound and knead
(put your muscle
into the work)
and pound again
and knead

into the tray
into the fire

let that heated air
bubble up inside
and rise

bubble up
and rise

so golden

fermenting the plate

the master
dreamed the leavening
of clays
through all
his waking hours

a sniff
nose wet
from the skimming water

finger dipped
into the residues

tasted

all the time
his dream
contorting
un-contorting

shifting its shape
between the smell
and the taste
to clay pastes
and white blocks

to the thick of it

pointing

> *this vat next*
> *it is ripe*

pointing

> *another month*
> *to stew*
>
> *maybe more*

stepping through the vapours
the mists
of a potter's breath
searching
for the next

the *ready*

aligning
what he sees
with all the minutes
of his waking hours

a union
of pallid porcelain

strength of porcelain

fired in the contained heat
a plate

a pretty thing

perhaps

but weak
from the trials of birth
by fermentation
and heat

a confusion

is it a thing of earth
or of water
perhaps
of fire

no no

the hole is dug
the plate is laid

a cup also

a vase
gently
on its side

sprinkle dirt

the raw dirt
to a level
where it is
truly
a burial

walk away

one month

two months

six months all up

the strength
of the named earth

the colour
of the new dirt
distilled in the hours
of darkness

beautiful
in its transparent strength

look through it
against the light
to see perfection

factory work

the factory was led
by the primary dreamer

her job
to see the way
using the vision
of the night

to tell —
with just a glance —
the true state
of the factory

of the way things
were

the way
they needed to be

the guard
stationed at the gatehouse —
an *unskilled* job —
was meant to receive

was *not* supposed
to judge

but every man
and woman
must present their poem
at the gatehouse

or else
no work

or else
no pay

or else no life
to warm their hearts
before the glare
of the red-eyed furnace

the unblinking fire

the guard
thought *madelaine* had progressed
the most
in the last few months
had high prospects

her verse
held form
and flow

a strict metre

pedro though
was still stuck inside
little doggy rhymes

not much

enough
for the right
to get a cheque
on payday

kenny —
the guard —
sometimes read aloud —
quietly —
a few of the stanzas
that he stole

down at the pub
in the parlour
with a pint of beer
when he was
by himself

Real Weight

all the time thinking

> *one day* . . .

> *one good day* . . .

he would write a poem
that he thought up
himself

on paper

and earn the right
to hand them in
to some other guard
while *he* worked
the better work
with the other skilled

in front of
the red eye
of the factory

under the sleeping hand
of the dreamer

the master dreamer

until then
he would accept
the scribblings and notes
of every working man and woman
who filed by him
to start their shift

and he would practice
by reading them
in a murmur

his lips moving
in the near silence
of an act of faith

stoking

    ooohh

    urhhh

    ooohh

    urhhh

as the furnace glows
the stoker
must work harder

every rise
in temperature
needs coal

    ooohh

another shovel

    urhhh

of coal

    urhhh

    ooohh

    urhhh
    urhhh

    ooohh

the stoker
is a man
made hard
by fire

Real Weight

    ooohh

toughened
hard baked
by flame

    urhhh

    urhhh

    ooohh

he shovels that coke
throws that coal
into the mouth
of the devil himself

    ooohh

    urhhh

the kiln devil

puts the fuel
into the guts
of the dance
of the devil

    ooohh

the stoker
is the temper
of fire

    urhhh

shaping class (no preconceptions)

*to make a shape
I must first make
no
shape*

*how –
you may ask –
can I make
'no shape'?*

watch me

I will show you

with that
he took clay –
very obviously moulded
into a round ball –
and attacked it

with both his hands
he kneaded
squashed
squeezed

pulled apart
and reunited

so hard
he went at his task
that a sheen of perspiration
prickled into existence
on his brow

when he had finished
what he held in his hands
was
a distortion
of what had been

Real Weight

now

he said
in a voice
that cracked
slightly
as he spoke

now
I can create

I can impose
my shape

to paint (like a master)

she wrote the brush
into her hand

within a paragraph . . .

the palette

using easy phrases
she expressed
an easel

the white paper

a little discomfited
at her own pretentiousness
she included the description
of a splotchy smock
she saw herself wearing

a beret
no not that
but
a loose hat
to keep the sun at bay
en plein air

lyrically
lovingly
she wrote a landscape

foreground:
trees
background:
blue and purple hills

clouds
across the sky

Real Weight

she paused
for a deep breath
like an olympian diver
perched up
on the high board

then
momentum resumed
she wrote
in a fever

> *the colours*
> *the hues*
> *the brush strokes*
>
> *the emergence*
> *of a corner*
> *of the centre*
>
> *of the borders*
>
> *the way the random*
> *transformed*
> *into shape*
>
> *depiction*

and the picture
that she wrote herself painting
was beautiful

worthy
to be hung
in a public place
for viewing

at the last
she wrote herself
penning her name —

the *artist's* name —
low down
in the left-side corner

and satisfied
she contemplated
how she might proceed
writing herself
a still life

a nude

perhaps a portrait

she wondered if —
next time —
she would do well
to write a *broader* palette
and a wider range
of colours

the fore-running dream (how to live an orderly day)

he would dream —
at night —
tomorrow

the day laid out
the tasks
lined up

the order
chosen and set

his
was a good sleep
a deep repose

and in the morning
the day took place
as he had dreamt it
with the tasks —
performed —
as laid out

the order
lined up

each thing
and its time
pre-chosen

his days passed
regularly

his mind . . .

a confident thing
relaxed and reposed

~

on the night
he did not dream . . .

> *the night*
> *that shared no vision*

> *the night*
> *that did not end*
> *with the daylight*

he could not rise
from his bed

he could not
do

did not know
how

> no repose

> no rest

> no sleep no dream

> no peace

how
would he *know*
what he must do

when
he had not seen it

he grew afraid
when a new night came

but sometime
in the deepest dark
he must have fretted
into a kind
of slumber

Real Weight

and he saw himself
then
the supplicant
in a pleading pose

and he felt the words
strike
as individual blows

>   *you are on your own*
>   *now*

different storm

she looked down
on a boiling sky

clouds filled up
with black

rain getting ready
to be given birth
in thunder

swirling
and whirling
growing like balloons
in dudgeon

lightning struck
rising *up* from the ground
to pierce
a pompous billow

and the water fell
drop by drop
turning cloud grey
turning cloud white
turning fat cloud thin
before her watching eyes

and the thunder rang out again

the lightning
flashed upwards
again

and so
the rain was born

tumble over tumble
birthed by the sky

to the ground

reverie of the woodman

it seemed as though
the first bite
of the axe
released
a dream

not from the log
but
from the man

and through the next
rhythmic
hour
as he swung
and struck

positioned

swung
and struck again

all the while
his cut billets
piling
in an irregular
and jagged
semicircle

like a wall
that he was constructing
deliberately

he drifted off
his thoughts
into a reverie

> *the naked wood*
> *all dressed*

*chopped and stacked
into neat rows
to head height
and under cover
from the weather*

*the lounge room
warm
on a raining day
of bitter cold*

*fire leaping
in the hearth
manic
in a flickering
that was danced solely
for his contentment*

swing
and strike

a last slice
removed from the round
added to the wall
as he automatically —
absently —
placed a fresh log
onto the block
and swung

and struck

by braille

she sculpted the head
with her hands

the size of it

the broad
shape

the weight

and by touch
she elaborated each eye

marked an iris

rounded a pupil

then
as though a blink
may one day be needed
she fashioned
for each
an eyelid

a nose
smooth geographical marker
of the landscape
that she felt
beneath her hand

nostrils curved
from *out*
to *in*

cheekbones
only visible
to her *touch*

her fingers explored —
so tactile —
the mouth

an excavation that then required
its own tongue
though silent
only ever speaking
into her head

she formed a ridge
inside . . .

etched the teeth

molars and canines

incisors

in the form of a smile
she added paired lips
full and rounded
slightly parted
as though paused
in the midst
of whispering
something profound

finally the ears

a canal
before the peculiar
contoured funnel
of the auricle

she built up
her sculpted head
from the inner
out

Real Weight

washed her hands clean
of remnant clay
and laid them —
once again —
gently
on the face

the hand

the hand
toward the sun
was over-large

it was bigger than
the arm
that held it upright

bigger
than the torso
folded in
upon itself

than the legs
arranged
in lotus

the closer
to the sun
the more pronounced
the disproportion

if it would go on
extending
it could cup
the golden orb
as though
in a cradle

or throw it
back
amongst
the other stars

yes
that hand
toward the sun
was
large

resistance

the stone was not
a yielding thing

it held
as strong in itself
as he was

though he pounded it
and though
he struck
all he gained
was powder and dust
where
his stone had stood . . .

the clay
was damp
it gave way to him
as he squeezed it

squashed it

it flattened out
then
curled around

embraced his fist

becalmed it
until he could not go on
with ire

there was no substance
to resist him

just a moving
embrace
and desire to be
the thing
that he needed

a little skunk

>*scat!*
>*scat!*

get yourself behind me

>(*scat! scat!*)

>*scat!*   *scat!*   *scat!*
>*scat!*

I say
get yourself behind me

you'd better
go

>(*scat! scat!*)

>(*scat! scat!*)

I turn myself around
put you
away beyond my shoulder

don't come too close
don't come too close

I've got the big guns

I will blaze you

>(*scat! scat!*)

all right all right
all right!

you're *really* looking for it

Real Weight

scat!

scat!

scat!   *scat!*   *scat! (take that)*

scat!

I said

    SCAT!

the beach

on the beach
named

    for dreamers

the sand
makes a moistened bed
for shells

coated
with *mother*
striated with colours —
pinks and browns
and greens —
they wait

and a dreamer
comes

lost
on his path
through the sundry shells
of potential dreams

seeing them all
seeing none of them
until . . .

there

is it the spiral

perhaps
it is the snail

a pipi
still with its pair

a scallop

Real Weight

maybe
an oyster —
rough —
or a black-blue mussel

he touches
a finger
to a shell

transfixed . . .

his eyes distort

he has been chosen

chosen

and now
the dream
begins

a viscous dough

no good will come
from kneading
wet

a sticky mess
is all

no good will come
from extra water

or even
honey

no good will come
for you will wear
your bread

a *damper* glove

all wasted

add
a little
flour —
do you hear me? —

add a little flour
do it
now

if you add
a little flour
the dough
will knead you
less

and bread
becomes a prospect
once again

Real Weight

if you add a little flour
if you *do*
just what I *say*

the dough
will leave your hands
and think
of rising

within the dough

the yeast —
the leaven —
will eat the dough

working it
from within

I —
poor fool —
have only hands
and fists

so I wait
for the bubble-rise

I wait
for the yeast

I wait
for an eruption
from the heart

and then I work
with a pounding
and I work with a punch

I push
turn it over
and I fold it

knead it
with my knuckles
I knead it
and I wait

wait

I wait
for the yeast
that is within

grounding of a poet by friend

oh
she is always there
with her head
in the stars

whether she sees
any more than the twinkle
who knows

I suppose
it is eternally clean
up
between the lights
and the darkness

maybe too pure
is what I'm trying to . . .

anyway
anyway

if you look
into her eyes
you'll get a faraway gaze
because
she *seems* to be here
but she's not
within miles

so
from time to time
I mix a bucket
of mud

and
from time to time
I take hold
of her hand

when I think
she's too far away

when I think she's been
too long gone

when I think
she might lose herself
in the tease of those
winking lights

I put her hand
in the slurry

I hold her
while she squirms

with her fingers
in the mud
I remind her
of earth

that she belongs
here
not lost in the stars

it's hard
to watch her
coming back
but it's what you do
as a friend

then she'll take a deep breath
and look me
in the eye

grunt a sort of

thank you

and cast around
for a pen

a pen
and a sheet of paper

Real Weight

lock herself in a room
and she'll write
where she's been

write
where the stars are

she'll write of her joy
of her broken heart
when she had to return

but
friends don't let friends
go
alone
among celestial bodies
out on astral planes

no friend
would do that

so I
accept the blame

yes
I accept her blame
and I would do it
for her
again

light (too heavy)

the dust he wrote
was lighter
than a touch
from the breeze

it filled the page
mote by mote
like swirling
in a ray of fallen sunlight
dazzling through
the window

dance . . .

his words could dance
for him
in rainbow colours
soft
as a blown breath

rain fell down
in the way rain
always will

the words grew heavy

caked with burden

dragging

slow

the rain fell down

dust into earth

earth
into mud

Real Weight

words
so
very
heavy

they danced no more

the sun returned
to bake the mud
good and hard

to hold the dust

to still
the delicate voice

hold the words

stasis

words
in stasis

.
.
.

the dust he wrote
was lighter
than the kiss
of a passing breeze

a voice of dust

she was made
from dust
turned into mud
with the aid
of water

crafted

she stood
just like
an animated person

did not speak
though truly
she would have liked to

her words
swirled into the air
like a rainbow of motes
adrift
without their meaning

but
her smile
was *made*
and
it was always
right there
sculpted
on her face

smiling
silently
always

she could dip
her head
as a way of greeting
but
when she attempted

Real Weight

> *hello*

when she *tried* to say
a soft

> *hello*

it was a cough
of small particles
released from her mouth

she knelt at night
raised her eyes . . .

a supplicant
at prayer

but
with no voice to speak
what god could hear
a dust cloud

a dry cough
a sneeze

and the dust
that she *was*
and that dust
that she still *is*
is the beginning
and the end

no one
has the right
to cry out
for more

and no god will hear
a mote
even though
it might make the sound
of weeping

closed: barefoot

he walked barefoot
in the mud
to feel himself
as one
with the moving earth

    mud

he said

    becomes hard dirt
    below the waterline

he closed his eyes

moved his toes

burrowed
a little deeper

felt the cool —
like a seeping
up
from the deep —
close over his feet

    close over

his arms
became so heavy
he could hardly . . .

    close over

the mud
is of the earth

Real Weight

it goes deeper
than the waterline

    welcomes

    embraces

    closes over

he walked barefoot
in the mud
to feel himself
as one
with the moving earth

    closed over

hammer/smith

a short
sharp
precise
blow by the hammer

a short
sharp
precise
exercise of her will

she glistens
gleams
in the flicker light
of the forge

and puts all
her heroic ferocity . . .

her unrestrained delight
into the short
sharp
precise
hammer strike
that sets the night
ringing

swirl dance

the flame dance is
sinuous

is
swirls

the flame dances
sinuous
in swirls

no straight line
no square
no right angle

the flame dances
sinuously

and
it swirls

halving the stone with love

the hammer strikes

a subtle touch

more
caress
than it is
a violence

a swift kiss
a lightning love

    there

and then
it is gone

the stone
in love's languor
is two halves

not yet
comprehending
it has been
broken

tuning

    c'lang

    c'lang

there is nothing
in place

only the bare surface
of the metal block

    c'lang

    c'lang

the strikes
of metal
upon metal
as the hammer
descends

    c'lang

are pre-emptive

    c'lang

soundings
and rangefinders

    c'lang

    c'lang

and so

the hammer
and
the anvil
have been tuned
before the day
is begun

now
let the work
flow

rules in the hands of the god (of war)

ya-ta-ta tah

ya-ta-ta

tah

here are the soldiers —
red arrayed —
on the heights
and all around
the hill

their colonels
and generals wear
special hats

they have artillery
aimed
primed
and ready

so ready

ya-ta-ta

ta-ta-ta

tah

here are the soldiers —
blue arrayed —
around the hill
up on the heights

their colonels
look jaunty
their generals wear
rakish hats

*such
rakish hats*

and their cannon
are loaded

> *their wicks lit*
>
> *the sparks
> sputter
> and hiss*

they are dressed well
for war

they look so smart
in the field

> *ya-ta-ta*
>
> *ta-ta-ta*
>
> *tah*

it is a shame
someone must lose
when turned out so . . .

[BANG]

the hammer
fell
upon the red

[BANG]

the hammer came d . . .

[CRASH]

. . . own on blue

Real Weight

the little boy laughed
at the chaos
below

and he laughed again

[BANG]

red

and again

[CRASH]

blue

he laughed

ya-ta-ta

ta-ta-ta

tah

and smote
with another swing
of his hammer

filled with

the silence . . .

filled with sound

I hear the blowfly
zzzumming

a tweet
from some small bird
is hardly
audible
at all

a lonely romeo —
occasionally croaking —
has set his home up
beneath a builder's wrap

a black plastic
auditoria

every now and

    croak

then

he sounds a heartfelt
loneliness

even silent
there is
the wind
that ruffles leaves
in trees
everywhere it passes

I hear it
yes
I do

Real Weight

it susurrates the silence

a near inaudible
song

I am
in full silence

filled with sound

three hammers

the watchmaker configures time
with tiny hammers
moved by cogs
pushed along by springs

the hands move
across the face
the hammer rears
like a serpent
in preparation

the spring
the cogs
the hands
the hammer

sound the hour

>   *dong*

>   *dong*

>   *dong*

mournful notes
that hang —
vibrating —
in the air

>   *dong*

>   *dong*

~

the carpenter measures
his lengths of wood
cuts them to size
with a trusty saw

Real Weight

aligns his joins
then
takes the big nail
from his tool bag

claw hammer
in his hand —
his good right hand —
he raises it
poised
to strike

without a beat
of hesitation
brings it down

    ah-wat

    ah-wat

    ah-wat

the echo sounds —
like a solid thrust —
the doubled-up cry

    ah-wat

~

in the cells
there are no tools
in reach

no tools
that a man *inside*
can use

but the need to strive —
the urge to respond —
is a driver

all through the night
and until the streaks
of dawn
he sounds
like a periodic gun

    a-augh

    a-augh

head bowed
till it touches the door

hands
in fists in the air

he hammers
in a rhythm

hammers
against the iron

past blood flow

    a-ugh

    a-ugh

he hammers at the door
with the smear
off his fists
beyond blood flow

    a-ugh

nerves of steel

you cannot jump

>**[jump]**

when the hammer
comes down

you must not
jump

>**[jump]**

when the hammer
comes down

the shaping block
is your training

the hammer
will instruct

you will learn . . .

you *must* learn
not to jump

>**[jump]**

>**[bang]**

the hammer
coming down

>**[jump]**

do not jump

>**[bang]**

the hammer
coming down

   [jump]

do not jump

(do not jump)

   [bang] [bang]

the hammer
crashing down

   [bang] [bang]

you will not jump

   [bang]

the block
is your training ground

   [bang] [bang]

you will not jump

reverie on a state (of being nothing)

stiller than still
is *being*

a state
that gathers *nothing*
in quantity

for the equation
of

    be
    don't
    do

nothing
happens *constantly*

massively

change is
the fire

fire
is the change

heat
is enough to turn
be
into
become

to turn nothing
into something
on the way
to something else

there is nothing
unchanged
in the fire

the craftsman
and his tools
renew
by pounding

    [blam]

    [blam]

so much
for nothing

    [blam]

so much for
unchanging

the forge
is not a place
for *being*

it is a place

    [blam]

for *making*

nothing
can *be*
again
after the heat
has passed

new tongs for the maker

as he ran the fresh
cold water
across the burn
to cool it —
as immediately
as possible —
he glanced down
at the patchwork
of discolorations
and old scars

the places where his thick
leather gloves
had not covered
or
where he had grasped
with foolishness

while drying the burn
gingerly —
before applying salve —
he visualised the work

always holding
a piece of metal

always too close
to the intense heat

hot tongs
holding super-hot
material

if only . . .

if only his hands
were not just flesh

if only they weren't so weak
and vulnerable
as he awkwardly
applied a dressing
to cover the abused flesh
and to protect it
he thought about tongs

why could his hands
not be *tongs* . . .

    always reliable

    useful

    able to get right up
    into the fire
    if that was needed

    if too hot
    then just needing to be dipped
    into the water trough

why could he not
have hands
that were
tongs

practical aids

he considered
as he patted down the plaster
now covering his wound

then went to the bench
where his pencils
and graph paper —
his instruments of drafting and design —
lay

he began to sketch an idea
for a new tool

tempering

an anguished cry —
more
a squeal
than scream —

unintentionally released

and then
the bubbling
hissing
seethe
of outrage

outrage!

the glowing iron
has met the water

there is temper

there is

silence

to appease

at the forge
she stoked the fire
with coal

in lumps

then
the bellows
wheezing

turning the black
to red
to fire so hot
she saw the devil

so hot
she gazed into the heart
of heat
dancing and singing
of hunger

with tongs
she thrust the rod
into the dance
until it glowed through red
to golden
and white

with the tongs
she paused a moment
above the water . . .

her small moment
of savour . . . .

anticipation

then she thrust

and then she thrust

Real Weight

*the rod
down
to bubble still water
with a hiss
and
with a scream*

her head
to hover
above the violent mist
that the rod of her forge
had turned to steam

a strange one —
she knew —
but she was aware
of the truth
about herself

a strange one —
but
the sound
and the storm
and the heated moist air
rising —
were soothing

when she opened her eyes
she had found
her own measure

peace
within herself

with her own devil

temporarily
an appeasement

the temper of steel

a deci of urine
rank
taken
from a he-goat

another deci of water
infused
by the juice
of two garlic cloves

allium sativa

ashes and lye

blue temper

a dip
of hot iron

a grey curse
of steam
that will scald

blue temper

hard steel

the cauteriser

raise the fire
good and hot

fan it
with the bellows

then put your metal
full length
in the middle
until it radiates

red
and orange

sun white

so white
you cannot stand it

when it has captured
all that fire

it is good

when it is holding
all that heat
it is good

quick now
move fast
take hold
of your beaten sword

douse it deep
into the cauteriser

let the water steam
and bubble
let the water
squeal

know
that the blue
that lines your blade
still holds the spirit
that was your flame

you hold
in your hands
the terrible fire

make you (like iron)

and he *was*
the sword

tempered in fire

drowned in water

born strong . . .

stronger

> *burn away*
> *burn away*
> *yesterday*
> *gone*
>
> *what you know*
> *lives in*
> *was*
> *not in*
> *is*
>
> *the fire will make you*
> *the water*
> *will set*
> *you*
>
> *you will be*
> *blue steel*
>
> *now*

hard and moral

weaknesses excoriated

will
forged like iron

paint your name

I will paint you
a picture

my paintbox
is filled with verbs
and adjectives

there is graphite
too
for a lead
in the pencil

my brush

let me start
now

I will apply the grey
to your name

I breathe a dancer

I breathe

a puff
onto the black

I breathe a puff

onto the black

I breathe . . .

a glow of red

I breathe a puff
onto the black

onto the red

my breath
onto a smoulder

into small smoke

I breathe a puff
into the red

into the gold

I breathe

a flame
of gold and red
and blue

I breathe

a dancer

the night forge

the orb
is on the pounding block

the darkness
in my hand
is pounding
night
upon the day

and the orb
glows golden
as it is heated

and the orb
grows rounder
as it is beaten

and gradually
recedes

.
.
.

blow by blow
descends

I smite —
one time again —
the light
that lingers

the night
is now alone

the fire
gone

necessary sacrifice

to give it strength
a lock of hair

the forge god took it
and grew hot

wove it —
with a song of fire —
into the metal

the precious metal

made it strong

and as the job
was done —
so bright and strong —
the smith
himself
grew weaker

faded

wan in the reflected light
of steel

outside
where the darkness lay
undisturbed

where no one looked
and
no one saw . . .

the quiet sound
of weeping

a vengeance

it was
a relationship
of
antagonism

nurtured
since she was a girl
and the anvil
even then
was aged
forever

hammer pounding

resistance

indifference

all the while
she grew
her size
her strength

in the days just past
she had forged
tempered
hardened
the metal of her vengeance

put her own essence
into the iron

now
she had
a *hammer*

she *was*
the new hammer
and her resentment
simmered over

Real Weight

swearing
inaudibly
beneath her breath
as she measured
for the blow

galling defeats . . .

grudging half-successes . . .

now

now

she raised the weapon
high
above her head
swung
with all that she was

crashed down
onto

into
the solid block

a mighty collision
that rang
and resounded
raising dust
and rattling walls
all through the forge

when she could see
she smiled

a gaudy rictus
through the black
caking on her face

the anvil lay
askew
in two parts

the rough of the middle —
the break point —
reflecting
like red diamond
the forge glow

she smiled
for a moment

then fell

rock-lan roll

he had heard
a rumour

so he took time
and studied
the land

he approached
a boulder
caught
in a state
of indecision

whispered
a slow word
in *rock-lan*

a weight
added
to a slow-growing
thought
held
in fine balance

he whispered
a slow
slow
word

and the boulder

rolled

chasm

a chasm
opened

wide

it took
a cloud

two

it opened wider
and drew in
a jet trail

a floating continent

and —
it opened wide
again —
a storm

raging lightning

strobe
and thunder
and wind

tempest
and swirl

it opened
wide

took them in

took in the blue
the light

a chasm
opened wide

Real Weight

it took in a cloud
or two

and then
it closed

the long dream

through the long night
it dreamed
of *height*

of wearing the clouds
as a necklace

as a beard

as a cool drink
of water

through the long night
it dreamed
of roundness

as perfect
as a ball
of hail

as smooth around
as a rainbow

a long night
of dreams

it dreamed a wind-shape

colours climbing

one
then another

etching
at the whim
of the wind

a long night to dream
of golden sand

Real Weight

washed clean
by water
moving

moving

shining in sunshine

rising in dust dance
to the passing
of a breeze

a long night

dreaming

the wind (on Easter Island)

the wind
persists

it has worn my face
away

so long
have I faced the ocean

so many storms
so many pounding seas

once
the movement was life
now
it wearies me

the third face
was silent
stoic
against the disfiguring erosion
of his features
and his senses

oh!

the sound
of a weight
an immensity
crashing
to the ground

oh

the remaining heads
as one
turned to face away

Real Weight

    the wind
          persists

spoken
into the earth

heard
as a rumbled murmur
felt
through the ground

hard rock

he wrote
about the rock

in words
chips and slivers
of defiance

hacking at it
with his ink
to create a spark
of connection
with that great
great
depth
of *hard*

but
nothing

.
.
.

dulled
blunted
maimed

limp . . .

nothing

his subject
wore him
down

sisyphus speaks

it is only
a rock

but close
like a brother

like a blade
against my skin

sometimes
I can almost feel
that I move
a colleague
capable
of feeling regret

sometimes
it is the ass
with hooves planted

nothing but stubborn
resistance
to whatever
I may do

some days
there is nothing
but a cold kiss
on my face

but
the rock must move

I
must roll it

and at the top

always
I sense a pleasure

the glee of a child
rolling

rolling to the bottom
of our mountain

ready to start
again

old (lithic) hurts

the stone shows signs —
on every side —
of birth
by gouge
by shear
and
by tearing

no wonder
it has failed to offer
a greeting

no wonder
it has grown hard
and deep
and true

it tolerates
my boots and stick
as I clamber
(so clumsy)

and gazes inward
nursing
its old stone pains

waiting

a long time waiting

to be healed

fred's backdrop

>it's only a play
>
>only a play . . .

he muttered
half to himself
half
to his silent listener

>only a play
>but
>every performance
>they want me
>to do a new backdrop

he began —
as he always began —
with a vast
black sheet

for paint
he had mixed pots
of his own formulae

plaster white
for the most part

>stars here . . .
>
>stars there . . .
>
>they've got no idea
>what star . . .

he carefully reached
to dab
near the centre
of the sheet

Real Weight

> *. . . what star*
> *goes where*
>
> *it amuses me*
> *from time to time*
> *to create . . .*

another reach
and dab

> *. . . the brand new*
> *constellation*
> *of* fred

he laughed
into a coughing
gurgle

sighed

the centrepiece —
or
off-centre piece tonight —
was to be a three-quarter
moon

looking cool
and distant

> *small*
>
> *last night . . .*

he breathed the words

> *I had to do it*
> *smaller*
>
> *tomorrow night*
> *they'll want it*
> *to be bigger*
> *again*

> *it changes*
> *every night*
> *fred*
>
> *just look at the script*

they tell him

> *only*
> *a bloody play*

he sat back
on his knees
and attempted to draw in
a mouthful of smoke
from the stub of a cigarette
permanently attached
to the side
of his lower lip

a last dab . . .

two

> *right*
> *that's done*
>
> *now*
> *give us a hand*
> *to get this up*
> *would you*
>
> *the show starts*
> *at sundown*

joyous

slew the rock

lava
stone

river red
running

choke the sky
grey the air

burn the flesh of the hapless
watching

world on fire

on fire

blow the top

dance
geyser
dance

ha ha
ha ha

dance
you geyser
dance

let the red rock
run
like slow water

hasty

seek the sea

hiss and blow

*bubble
the water*

call it home

*call this
home*

rest a while

*call it
home*

oneiric research (preparing to dream)

she obtained books
sent away
orders

for listings
advertised in catalogues

scoured library network
for informed works
on the subject

and she read

made notes

cross referenced
and indexed

she studied
until her mind held
everything it could hold

only then —
weary soul —
did she seek out
the down
in the doona

the feather-soft
of the pillow

only then —
when she knew all —
was she ready
to sleep

and perhaps
to dream

murmur

sometimes —
all caught up
in a shell —

the sound
is of the ocean

shushing
the ear
like the water

the wave
and the tide

sometimes —
if I cup my hand

hold it to constrain
my hearing —

sometimes . . .

those times

I can hear
the murmur
of my dreams

Real Weight

the miner reflects on his mountain deep

*it is a long way
down
when you know
that
there's a half a mile
of dirt
and rock
above you*

*and the space you've carved –
for yourself to move –
is only two men
wide*

*you have to
shore
your tunnels*

*keep the pump
primed
and pushing out water*

*keep the light
on your helmet
alive*

*I
went down there*

*pick-axe
in my hand
and no concern
for risk
or for danger*

*breathing black
shitty dust
in the eternity
of black
shitty night
where
I could not see
my hand*

there

right before my eyes

*and my ears filled up –
down there –
with god*

*god
choosing that deep time
to start talking*

*but I plinked
and I plunked
with my pick
and did my best
to keep his voice
outside
of my head*

*because I needed clear mind
for the work*

*it is a soul
down there*

some kind of spirit

*I'd sit down
on a break . . .*

no light

Real Weight

no sound at all
but my breathing
and
I could see –
I swear –
six different kinds
of blackness

the working
of a heart
is a loud call
too

its sound
is a determined beat
and the sound of mine
would fill all the tunnels
right up
with me

like a claim I'd staked
but
I didn't really
belong there

I didn't own
any part of that creature
I only
stole

I stole all the ore
that ever gleamed
or glittered
in my light

and –
thief though I was –
I don't think the mountain
squatting up there
above me
ever even knew
that I was alive

I stole the ore out

*I was a miner
and a thief
but
half a mile down —
somehow —
I learned
to pray*

colours of the great work

my *Great Work*
is black and white
and red

black to grey
Mercury
to *Saturn*

the Philosopher says
Lead
but I care nothing
for *The Wise*

Jupiter
in the water
Venus
in a shell

Moon becomes *The White*
Venus
dons gold

Mars –
her friend –
is *Red*
until *The Dawn*

my *Great Work*
is black
and white

and red

introvert medicine

Sun	Gold	Heart
Moon	Silver	Brain
Saturn	Lead	Spleen
Mars	Iron	Gall
Venus	Copper	Kidney
Mercury	Mercury	Lung
Jupiter	Tin	Liver

I am physician
to the sun

to your heart

silver
to your brain . . .

the moon
waking you
at night

introvert medicine

the planets
are at play

with your body . . .

liver and lungs

copper
for a kidney
iron
in the gall

I am physician
to precious metals
and the stars

introvert physician
to you

bridging mine

in bridging the distance
between
precious stone
and
precious star

I established
the necessary correspondence
linking
the thing I touched
with
the thing
I saw

I held one
to the light

I beheld
another
that was shining

a constellation
in my hand

an untapped lode
sparkling
above my eyes

the incomplete findings of the dream reviewer

the dream –
from the outside –
appeared both
stock
and standard

there seemed to be
something going on
involving the usual
illogical absurdity

so *typical*
of a dream

>*the tree commanded*

>*a sun*
>*rose*

>*the tree commanded*

>*a forest*
>*burst into leaf*

>*into flower*

>*the tree commanded*

>*a new season*
>*came into being*

>*the tree invited*

>*the universe drank*
>*from its coursing sap*

ridiculous stuff
that you always see
when watching a dream

Real Weight

the investigator –
engrossed
in the writing
of her report –
failed
to notice
the drift –
closer –
of the dream
she had been studying

did not see
a wooden hand –
trailing fibrous tendrils
of root and hair –
reach out
from the enclosing bubble . . .

seized suddenly –
fiercely –
by the arm

she was held

encompassed

incorporated

into the splendour
of the realm

where
the tree . . .

the *one* tree

could make a sun
shine

diamond and star

>*what
>is to say . . .*

he spoke
as though addressing
an auditorium

>*. . . what is to say
>a diamond
>is not
>a star?*

his pause
was a flourish

theatrical
though perhaps
wasted

>*bear with me*
>
>*a star shines*
>
>*to the unaided eye
>it is
>as a diamond
>of light*
>
>*glints may be seen
>to be reflecting
>away
>from the stellar
>facets*
>
>*who
>has not seen
>the rays of light
>radiating out?*

Real Weight

and the diamond?

well
shine a light
at a diamond
in the darkness

then tell me . . .

again he looked
to the far corners

> *. . . tell me*
> *that it does not*
> *shine*
>
> *like*
> *a star*

.
.
.

his audience –
which comprised
myself alone –
thought about it

> *ohh*
> *yeah . . .*

I said

> *. . . it does*
>
> *a bit*

the contemplation

he lit
the last cigarette
of the night

watched the glow

>*fierce
>at the tip*

>*and peppered with crackle
>as he dragged in
>air
>and smoke*

>*a grey-white length
>of ash
>accumulated*

>*extended*

>*horizontal
>at first
>just like the cigarette
>that it had been*

>*then
>sagged*

>*waiting for the right
>moment
>of breeze
>or tremor
>to
>fall*

>*at the same time
>blue smoke
>rose
>from the burning end*

Real Weight

*seductively rising
as a translucent colour
seeking the sky*

weightless

buoyant

*gradually
losing its form
and breaking
into a dancing line
of twists
and wavers*

before dispersing

he watched
the ash

he watched
the smoke

contemplated
weightlessness
and
gravity

the suddenness of a change (of voices)

the voice
had been the mid-throat
of shouted warning

even as it became
louder –
higher in pitch –
it faded
away

less than
a heartbeat
rendered it
up there

less than
another
till it was
gone

replaced
by a rush of sound
like an audible
buffet
of the wind
rising
to mock
and to taunt

and to whistle

where *I* may be

I am
somewhere

I feel
nothing

only air
to resist me

air
that feels like . . .

nothing

no
resistance

only *me*
moving my arms
and legs

at least . . .

I *think* so

I may be going –
flowing –
in a forward
kind of way

I *may* be holding
my position

in a stasis

moving but
not moving
at all

this *nothing*
has
no colour
or
I am blind . . .

yes

I am
blind

up
is somewhere

perhaps
it is for *me*
to nominate

to dictate
the horizon

declare north
of it

is north
of it?

south
some other
where

lying on my back
I am . . .

or
on my belly

there seems no way
that I
can *know*

though
it also seems
that I *am*
somewhere . . .

Real Weight

maybe
rising

I would like
to think . . .

perhaps

that I
am rising

Bachelard Source Materials

Gaston Bachelard, French Philosopher lived from 27 June 1884 to 16 October 1962. The series of poems and poetry in this book has drawn inspiration from the following publications by Bachelard, translated into English.

Intuition of the Instant by Gaston Bachelard (1932) Eileen Rizo-Patron (Translator) Northwestern University Press, 2013

The New Scientific Spirit, by Gaston Bachelard (1934), A. Goldhammer (Translator) Beacon Pr; 1st Edition (1984)

The Psychoanalysis of Fire, by Gaston Bachelard (1938), A.C. Ross (Translator) (1964).

Lautréamont, Gaston Bachelard (1939), Robert S. Dupree (Author), James Hillman (Author), Dallas Institute Publications; Reprint Edition (2012)

Water and Dreams: An Essay on the Imagination of Matter by Gaston Bachelard (1942), Edith R. Farrell (Translator) (1983.

Air and Dreams: An Essay on the Imagination of Movement, by Gaston Bachelard (1943), Edith R. Farrell (Translator), Frederick Farrell (Translator) Dallas Institute Publication Dallas Institute Publications (1988)

Earth and Reveries of Will: An Essay on the Imagination of Matter by Gaston Bachelard (1943), Kenneth Haltman (Translator) Dallas Institute Publications (2002)

Earth and Reveries of Repose: An Essay on Images of Interiority by Gaston Bachelard (1948), Mary McAllester Jones (Translation), Dallas Institute Publications (2011)

Dialectic of Duration. Gaston Bachelard (1950), Mary McAllester Jones (Translator), Rowman & Littlefield Publishers; (2016)

The Poetics of Space by Gaston Bachelard (1958), Maria Jolas (Translator) Penguin Classics (1964).

The Poetics of Reverie, by Gaston Bachelard (1960), Daniel Russell (Translator) Beacon Press; New Ed Edition (1971)

The Flame of a Candle, by Gaston Bachelard, (1961), Joni Caldwell (Translator) Dallas Institute Publications (1988).

The Right to Dream by Gaston Bachelard (1970), J.A. Underwood

(Translator) Dallas Institute Publications (1988)
Fragments of a Poetics of Fire, by Gaston Bachelard, Kenneth Haltman (Translator), Dallas Institute Publications (1988)
On Poetic Imagination and Reverie, by Gaston Bachelard, Colette Gaudin (Translator) Spring Publications; (2014)

Author Information

Frank Prem has been a storytelling poet since his teenage years. He has been a psychiatric nurse through all of his professional career, which now exceeds forty years.

He has been published in magazines, online zines, and anthologies in Australia, and in a number of other countries, and has both performed and recorded his work as spoken word.

He lives with his wife in the beautiful township of Beechworth in North East Victoria, Australia.

Connect with Frank

Find Frank at his website www.FrankPrem.com, or through Social Media online at Facebook, X (Twitter), Instagram and YouTube.

Other Published Works

Free Verse Poetry

Small Town Kid (2018)
Devil In The Wind (2019)
The New Asylum (2019)
Herja, Devastation - With Cage Dunn (2019)
Walk Away Silver Heart (2020)
A Kiss for the Worthy (2020)
Rescue and Redemption (2020)
Pebbles to Poems (2020)
The Garden Black (2022)
A Specialist at The Recycled Heart (2022)
Ida: Searching for The Jazz Baby (2023)
From Volyn to Kherson (2023)
Alive Is What You Feel (2023)
White Whale (2024)
Pilgrim Volume 1 - Illustrated by Leanne Murphy (2024)
A Poetry Archive Volume 1 (2024)
A Poetry Archive Volume 2 (2024)
A Poetry Archive Volume 3 (2024)
A Poetry Archive Volume 4 (2024)

Picture Poetry/Spoken Image

Voices (In The Trash) (2020)
The Beechworth Bakery Bears (2021)
Sheep On The Somme (2021)
Waiting For Frank-Bear (2021)
A Lake Sambell Walk (2021)
A Few Places Near Home (2023)
The Cielonaut (2024)

What Readers Say

Small Town Kid

A modern-day minstrel. Highly recommended.
—A. F. (Australia)

Small Town Kid is a wonderful collection.
—S. T. (Australia)

Devil In The Wind

Trust me, this book will stay with you. Bravo!
—K. K. (USA)

Moving, beautiful, and terrible. I was left with a profound sense of respect, as well as a reminder that we should never take for granted every precious every moment of life.
—J. S. (South Africa)

The New Asylum

Words can't do justice to the emotional journey I travelled in (reading this collection).
—C. D. (Australia)

If I had to pick one book over the past year that has truly resonated with me, this would be it.
—K. B. (USA)

Walk Away Silver Heart

Instantly grips you by the throat in his step-by-step story of survival. Bravo!
—K. K. (USA)

Outstanding!
—B. T. (Australia)

A Kiss For The Worthy

A Celebration of Life Written in Thoughtful Bursts of Poetic Expression
—C. M. C. (United States)

With every verse, I found myself reflecting about myself, my life, and the world.
—K.

Rescue and Redemption

The passion of love in its many forms explored by one for another.
—J. L. (United States)

I've enjoyed every word, every breath. Every moment within the life of these stories.
—C. D. (Australia)

Sheep On The Somme

Museums and archivists take note--sell this in your gift shops, preserve it in your archives. Professors, teachers--share with your students.
—A. R. C. (United States)

(This) book is a beautiful and graphic tribute to all those brave men and women who gave their lives for their countries between 1914 and 1918.
—R. C. (South Africa)

Ida: Searching for The Jazz Baby

I found myself deeply moved by the presentation of Ida's elusive, illusionary life.
—E. G. (United States)

He gives her a depth and vulnerability that the press didn't.
— A. C. (United Kingdom

The Garden Black

Prem creates verse that illuminates our world, its experiences and history.

—S. C. (United Kingdom)

Prem's poetry reminds that life is fragile and fleeting ... both harsh and beautiful.

—D. G. K. (Canada)

A Few Places Near Home

The author has captured many beautiful images in this book, and is a wonderful photographer as well as a poet. This book would make a beautiful coffee table book filled with moving prose to make us ponder with gorgeous accompanying images.

—D. K. (Canada)

www.FrankPrem.com

www.ingramcontent.com/pod-product-compliance
Lightning Source LLC
Chambersburg PA
CBHW050157130526
44590CB00044B/3377